Reclaim Your Subconscious Mind

Reclaim Your Subconscious Mind

Take control of your life using the power of your mind

Marie Ireland

Reclaim Your Subconscious Mind
Copyright © Marie Ireland 2012, 2013, 2014
First published January 2014

The author asserts the moral right to be identified as the author of this work.

ISBN 978-0-473-27618-8

All rights reserved. No part of this book may be reproduced, stored in a retrieval system, or transmitted in any form or by any electronic or mechanical means including photocopying, recording, information storage and retrieval systems, or otherwise, without prior permission in writing from the author, with the exception of a book reviewer, who may quote short excerpts in a review.

To order copies of this book please visit www.1-desire.com www.amazon.com or www.createspace.com

Also available as an ebook on www.amazon.com

Printed by CreateSpace

Dedication

To my readers

*My sincere intention in writing this book is
to help you in any way I can,
through my experiences and the knowledge I can share with you.*

*I have applied this knowledge to my life
and am always continually achieving positive results,
so I hope you can also be inspired
to achieve your dreams.*

Acknowledgements

I would like to thank my parents Vern and Rosie for providing me with a strong foundation and giving me so much unconditional love, support and patience as I went through my life experiences.

Also to my siblings, Brian, Paula and Diane, in being the best brother and best sisters one could ask for. They have always supported me and each other unconditionally. Our parents taught us kindness and honesty, and these are the most valuable things we have all learnt. As we have this kindness deeply ingrained in our being, everything we do is always for the higher good. I could not have asked for a better gift than what my parents gave me, and I am so very grateful. With this gift I endeavour to help others for I will always only create and share for the higher good for humanity.

I must thank Bob Proctor. The gifts that he lives by and shares with the world have inspired me to live out my own destiny. I admire him mostly because he is a pure example of an honest, unconditional giver with the greatest integrity.

I also want to thank all those in my life who have inspired me to grow and create the life of my dreams. I am so very grateful for every person and every experience I have encountered and even more grateful for the difference I can make for humanity.

With gratitude,
Marie

CONTENTS

Dedication   *v*
Acknowledgements   *vi*
Preface   *ix*

MY EXPERIENCE   1

CHAPTER 1   17
Introduction   17
Laws of the Universe   30

CHAPTER 2   39
Thought Forms   39
The Power of Your Conscious and Subconscious Mind   42

CHAPTER 3   49
Live In The Moment   49
Time   54
Your Soul Essence   58

CHAPTER 4   61
Health, Consciousness and the Subconscious Mind   61
Healthy Boundaries   64

CHAPTER 5   73
The Power of Desire, Imagination and Emotions   73
How to Manifest through Emotions and Imagination   78

CHAPTER 6   83
Prepare to Change Your Life and Discover Your Hidden
    Self-sabotage/Paradigms   83
Learn From What is Going Wrong   85
Be Unrealistic and Realistic at the Same Time   87

Preface

We live in a world of uncertainty, frustration, relationship issues, challenges in moving forward in life, attaining material wealth or trying to find that one person we want to spend the rest of our life with.

I know you may have heard it all before but have you really understood?

When you do understand, you can recognise that you 'attract' everything in your life, which will pull you further in the direction of your desires. So reading this book will be significant for your growth and what you require to know and learn. You have 'attracted' this book for a reason, and I believe I can answer your nagging questions in a simplistic way so you can begin the transformation into the life you desire.

You must need assistance in some area of your life to have been drawn to this book. When we feel we understand everything and know it all, this is when we need to ask ourselves to open our minds even more, because learning and growing is unlimited. We not only need to know, but we must understand and then apply what we have learnt. There is no point saying 'yes I know all this', because, to date, you have not actioned it. When we do find ourselves saying 'I already know' before we delve further, then right away we are blocking our consciousness to receive more growth.

You see, there is growth in everything on different levels. If you are watching or reading something over and over, your consciousness will have a different perception of it every time. This perception is the key to expanding your consciousness. In saying this, I have a gift for you in this book, or you would not have attracted what I am about to share with you, and some special messages of your inner knowing (a part of your higher intelligence) which have been there all along but merely forgotten.

I hope my book will be the beginning of some significant changes for you. Use it as you see fit. It will help you find your own answers and guide you as to how to go about progressively moving forward. We will cover a range of topics so you can form a full picture of how everything in relation to you interlinks and creates cause and effect. As you progress, you might feel I am repeating myself; however, I use different wordings so your conscious mind can read it from different points of view to help you understand it further. It is important for you to see the whole picture clearly.

My book has many answers as to why we believe what we do and how our beliefs and habits control our lives. Don't get me wrong – of course you have your own truth and choose what is right for you and your journey in life, but if you keep an open mind you can recognise patterns throughout your life and see areas that need change. You will then find where your thoughts and beliefs have held you back – probably because they were most likely never really your own thoughts in the first place. I will explain in depth as we proceed.

Before you make any judgment while reading I suggest you keep an open mind as you go. So read carefully and take what information you feel is right for you. I hope you will most likely feel right at home. If not, perhaps question what has brought you to read my book, because a huge part of you is in need of change. If you are having challenges in life then I absolutely believe that I can help you understand why and how to change it once and for all.

The foundation of your existence is realising you are one
with a great source
of ultimate abundance and everything
is in direct connection with you.

You alone have the power to bring this abundance towards you
if you can allow yourself to believe and open up to all possibilities.
To truly understand and know that
everything is in connection with you,
your subconscious is the key
to truly experiencing everything your heart desires.

In summary, I would like to share my story with you as it is relevant to why I was so inspired to write it and share this knowledge. I will be as brief as possible – you are of course reading this to better *your* life and to find *your* life purpose. I have had my fair share of challenges, but I will not delve into them all. It is now about *you* making a connection with your life's challenges, understanding how you also can influence the outcomes in your life. My examples and destructive experiences will help you relate to the challenges in your own life.

I have gone through life unaware of my dysfunction and how my life continued on a downward spiral even though I tried to start over again and again and again. It felt like a never-ending battle.

This may seem like any other self-help book, but it is not just that. I have explained things in a simple way so you can identify easily where you would fit in with it, and I have a free workbook to help you identify even further exactly what you want to change in yourself and your life. I also want you to feel you can make contact with me if you require further assistance or have any questions. Now, let's begin.

My Experience

I was born in 1972 with a small challenge. I had club feet, which were turned inward so badly the doctor told my parents if they did not operate my ability to walk would be severely impaired. Nowadays they can fix club feet quite easily. Even though it was not a life-threatening challenge, it was a journey that still impacted my life.

My life then unfolded in a negative direction seeming to emanate from something I had learnt about myself, which was in fact an illusion, and how I thought I fitted into this world, from the moment I was born. What I mean by illusion is a false sense of image, and this is what controlled the way I thought and how I made decisions in life.

At the age of only six weeks I was admitted to hospital. This, as I understood, became a huge challenge for my parents and my older brother who was only two years old. At that time parents were not allowed to stay in the hospital with their children, no matter what age the child. This is a fragile time, and for a newborn to be separated from its parents is not a natural process. The whole situation had an effect on me that caused negative emotions. These emotions related to feeling alone and afraid, and also I formed an emotion of guilt I have carried for 40-odd years. Because I am aware of this feeling I can transmute it just by recognising this illusion, which I have held on to. My parents felt guilty they had to leave me in the hospital even though they could not do anything about it. So whenever they felt upset about anything in their life I automatically felt guilty, despite their feelings having nothing to do with me. It was an automatic conditioning I had developed at a very young age. There is a valid reason for this and how it happens. I will explain further in the later chapters.

I continued to be in and out of hospital for seven years. There was one significant time in hospital which I clearly remember – being in the operating theatre, lying on the operating table. At one point I remember looking over the doctors performing surgery on my legs and then I woke up. I was conscious but I could not feel any pain! In that moment, as I realised I was lying on the table, I struggled to open my eyes, probably because of the sleeping drugs, but I forced them open to let them know I was awake. When the anaesthetist saw my movement she placed the mask over my face and of course I went back to sleep.

For years I had no real understanding of what happened then; however, I have been told by a couple of highly experienced spiritual healers that I had in fact temporarily died on the operating table, which explains two instances that occurred. The first was that I was watching myself on the table being operated on, and the second was that I had woken up, which relates to my soul coming back into my body at a faster rate causing my body to wake while still in surgery. I had been told the soul can travel fast to the body when it wants to reconnect to the physical, and the speed in reconnection is what activated my body to wake at that moment. It is never something I have researched as it never interested me to do so, but I do know that was what I had experienced.

Over time in my young life dealing with the medical profession, I could not bear to go near hospitals. When I did have to go back to get my plaster taken off, I screamed the place down on every visit. All they were doing was cutting off my plaster, a basic procedure. Can you imagine the look on the doctors' faces when they heard my outrageous screams! I particularly remember one time - which seems funny now - I was sure the doctor was going to cut my leg when removing the plaster. I realise this fear was caused by my waking on the operating table. In general, my experience created an overarching fear of being ill as it meant doctors and hospitals.

I want to explain a little about my personal experience and how I interacted with the outside world.

Throughout my childhood I use to notice the way people were functioning in life. Not that I had learnt anything about life and the reasoning for people's actions, etc. I was still only a small child, but I remember being very opinionated and knew exactly what I was saying I believed was true. I don't know how I knew it but I just knew. At the time I could never work out why they did not listen to me and how they did not know this. I used to wonder why they would continue to do things in such a way or see things the way they did. I was a child who often asked questions, and this behaviour annoyed others. I could not work out why everything seemed dysfunctional and life seemed difficult for everyone. I also could not understand why things had to be certain ways and why people thought things were right. I began to be very curious and frustrated with a lot of things and people. I did not want to accept how life was, as I believed that is not how life was meant to be. I felt like an adult in my little body, which sounds weird, and I felt others didn't really want to listen to my opinion. This did not seem to stop me expressing my truth because I knew it was true in my heart. My own questions arose during my life but I began to find the answers through my life experiences.

As I grew older I used to think to myself: *One day I will be in a position where I can impact the world for the higher good.* This was what I believed I could do, and this is what I wanted to do so much, even though I did not know how. I knew I had a special purpose because of how differently I thought to everyone else. I never felt like I fitted in properly anywhere, even though I felt very secure at home with my own family, but I still had a different perception on life and this is what used to frustrate me.

We were fortunate children as we had a very loving family and great parents who always made sure we were taken care of. They were always concerned for our well-being and would do anything for us. But my parents worked hard all the time to give us security and provide the family with what we needed.

I would feel sad and get upset to see people unhappy, and I so much wanted to fix and change things for our whole family. It saddened me that my parents would have to work so hard. It is something that never stopped, and I formed a strong desire in my heart that I wanted to be able to give them everything they deserved so they could have an easier life. To me this was not how life was to be lived. And I resolved that I was not going to live my life as they had to.

As a young child my strongest desire was to create a life that will give freedom to my family because I felt and thought differently from others, and it seemed like I did not fit in properly anywhere. I then became self-conscious over my opinions, as they always seemed to cause a reaction. I was very sensitive and got hurt a lot by outside influences. I also became self-conscious because my feet and legs were so different. I used to have to wear special boots and steel bars on my legs, which reached up to my knees, and I had to wear those pretty much 24 hours a day – even in my sleep because it helped my feet grow in the correct position. I suffered pain and discomfort from the pressure of the boots, and because of them it became obvious I was different in others' eyes. I often felt sorry for myself.

I did not have many friends. I never really knew why, so I put it down to the fact I was not good enough because of my point of difference. Of course a child would do this regarding its insecurities. Deep inside my heart, I had a dream that one day I would be able to help people be happy. I could see that people used to talk so harshly and unkindly, it just didn't seem right to me. I don't know why I thought this – I just knew I needed to have a voice and to be heard. Over time I came to understand that adults thought they knew better just because they were older. In a way I took on others' advice even though a part of me felt something quite different.

At the age of 21, I was diagnosed with rheumatoid arthritis. I would not accept what the doctor told me and refused to take anything he prescribed and went to a naturopath the next day. She tested me for food allergies and told me I had a high intolerance to milk. The lactose in the milk had crystallised in my joints. I followed her advice and replaced the milk by soy milk, and within only two days my strength came back and I no longer had any pain. It was a wonderful feeling to be able to cure myself in this way without medication.

Over a few years I slowly started to eliminate dairy from my diet, as I realised it was an unhealthy food to consume.

Within this same year of this small health set back I had been unfortunate as my boss was dishonest about my hairdressing apprentice. I was told I was signed up in a hairdressing apprenticeship, but in fact my hours of work were not going towards my qualifications at all.

I worked hard for that person and found I was progressing fast with my skills. I was confident I was going to pass all my exams. Little did I know I would never be able to take those exams. For the past 18 months I had been working towards being a fully qualified hairdresser but when the time to sit my exams was near I realised I was not getting any papers to prepare and sign off.

After getting no response from my boss I took control and contacted the right people. I discovered I did not exist on their records. This was a huge shock, and I could hardly believe it. I arranged for them to come to the salon to discuss it with my boss. The rest was messy and, long story short, I took her to the small claims court, but I could not attain any hours towards my apprenticeship because nothing had been recorded on my training over this time. However, because I was underpaid but not legally an apprentice, she had to compensate me for loss of pay. This did not make up for it at all, as I wanted the hours recorded towards my training time.

I was saddened by this occurrence and decided to leave the city, and I felt so disheartened I gave up my hairdressing career. All I wanted to do was move away. I felt betrayed and hurt that someone could do that to me and especially when they pretended to be a friend. So I began my life in a different town. I tried to go back into hairdressing at one point but I did not trust anyone so I decided to let go.

Over the next seven years I struggled with my direction and had relationship challenges. It became a huge learning curve, and it didn't seem to really end. I also struggled to find true friends, which had always been a challenge for me.

I moved town again with my partner at the time when we were going to start a new life. I decided I did want to get back into hairdressing. I got a job with a great place; however, not long after, I discovered I wanted to open my own business. So I set out to create the salon I wanted. Clients began following me and I started to build up a great clientele. Things were hard at first as any business is but I continued to push through as my hairdressing ability gave me the confidence that I made people feel happy and wonderful about themselves. This is what pushed me to want to do better. I loved how I made people feel.

After a few years my life took a turn for the worse. I noticed I began to have health challenges so I decided to move my salon. I built a salon underneath my parents' investment house, which I rented from them. This became an expensive project but I felt it was a more advantageous transition that allowed better business cash flow and less stress.

I still continued through life with many challenges relating to health, relationships and career.

With all my challenges I began to turn towards a spiritual calling. I felt like I had been disconnected from my true nature and 'knowing', which I had as a child. I began realising I had been extremely challenged in my life because of this disconnection. I had met a spiritual guru and from him I learned a lot about myself. After I reconnected and became more in touch with my own soul and finding my way with my higher self, other things began to happen.

It was as if there were changes in my life to be made even though I was not sure how these changes would occur. I was not even sure *what* changes needed to happen but knew I could not go on as I was.

At the age of 28, after only six months of working from home, I got chemical poisoning, viral meningitis, a brain aneurism and went through early menopause. The early menopause I didn't discover until a few years later. I had had medical examinations to confirm I had gone through the change of life at a very rapid rate, due to my body going through a health shock, as well as having a rare hormone gene. This gene triggered the hormonal shift after excessive trauma to the body. The diagnosis was a huge shock to me as I hoped one day I would have children. It took me a couple of years to pass a point of acceptance and, mostly because of the hormonal change, I no longer had this desire.

I began to experience huge miracles – the first saved me from the brain aneurism. I was put in touch with a special healer who placed a poultice on my head and pulled the blood clot out through the pores of my skin. Now you might find this hard to believe, and most people would have to see it to believe it. But it is 100 per cent factual. Only 10 minutes after the healer applied this poultice, my pain disappeared. And the most amazing thing, after a few hours' process, the healer removed the poultice, and I could physically see that it had absorbed the blood clot exactly from the area where I felt pain. It was a miracle healing for me, and I felt truly blessed to have received it. He had saved my life, and I will always be grateful to him and that experience.

Another challenging time was one night when I was in extreme emotional distress. I was crying from my soul, and I experienced receiving the direct connection with our divine energy. This will always be something special for me. It started with strong emotional pain in my heart, and it became an uncontrollable emotional release, as if my whole life of experienced emotions had come to the surface. It became so overwhelming I had no choice but to surrender and allow the feeling to flow out of me. I cried from the core of my being, and my emerging emotion just kept on coming. I cried and cried.

I have never had physical tears when I cry, but that night they were pouring out of me.

When I was in the middle of my release, a light shone through the partially open door and caught my eye. I got up, thinking the light had been left on, but when I got to the doorway there was nothing there. I returned to bed but the same light caught my eye again, except it was very bright, and moving. In that moment I thought someone was in the hallway with a torch but what I was about to witness was incredible.

From my side of the door I could see the light was becoming more concentrated, making it brighter, then again it came closer to the doorway.

If you can imagine a comet with a tail, this is exactly how the energy moved into my room, bounced from the side of the bed and hovered up into the left side of the room, just waiting there. The room was an unbelievable, glowing haze. The peace that washed over me was so serene, and I felt amazingly gifted from this presence. When I acknowledged the reason for the presence, the spirit left. This event changed my life, as I had gone through a direct connection with our Universal Energy and divine wisdom. I felt honoured to be in such a powerful presence. There is nothing more powerful than receiving the divine energy in our physical world. This presence felt so familiar to me, and I knew it was the truth of what I believed in my heart when I was a child.

Little did I know but only a few weeks later I was about to come up against more heartache and life's troubles than I had never experienced before. I had been through all sorts of dramas in my life, and it seemed they happened one after the other. I won't go into them as they involve other people, but I will say that one of the hardest times was when my heart was completely broken. I could not believe how much pain I felt from a broken relationship, and how extremely betrayed. I only had about two hours sleep per night for a few weeks, and this took its toll on my body – chemical poisoning, viral meningitis and brain aneurism. It was exhausting. But the biggest challenge of all was the fact I had experienced a broken heart when I was already worn out. I was completely devastated.

This was the most difficult time in my life and especially while I barely had enough strength to deal with overcoming all these health challenges I was facing.

The most important thing I always remembered through my emotional struggle was to pray and ask my divine spirit to be there for me and help me be strong. Just when I needed to have something positive happen, I experienced the opposite. I did not think things could get much worse but they were about to.

Not long after my heartbreak something horrible happened. An unstable stalker was invading my space at home for a number of weeks. It was terrifying. The police became involved, but it was difficult to pinpoint his timing and action. Long story short, I decided to move out of the area into a safer environment.

From my past relationship breakup I continued to grieve from my broken heart, and it took me about two years to release the pain from this hurt.

Throughout this ordeal and after, I felt like I was floating through life and had no real direction or focus. It was as if I just had to find a way to heal every part of my soul, body and life. I used to express my inner feelings by writing lyrics to help myself heal. I continued to be challenged with health problems, not only because of my past health issues but more so now that emotional stress was playing a huge part in my life. Even though it took two years for the heart pain to stop, it took me approximately 10 years to be released from the impact I allowed this person to have on my life. It took so long because I had to go through so much emotional shock, and this you will understand later on as I explain how emotions have such a strong hold on our mind and in our life.

At the age of 39 I was diagnosed with auto immune disorder, then the rheumatoid arthritis returned again. I was told I had suffered from auto immunity for years without realising. This is when the body starts attacking itself. I realised it signified I was emotionally and mentally attacking myself for all the trauma I had put myself through. I started to blame myself and internalise my experience. This began taking a toll on my health, as I did not know how to change until I recognised that I began my life going in and out of hospital and therefore most of my life was impacted by health challenges. I went through victim consciousness, blaming others for my hurt, and then I realised my insecurities created a lot of issues in my life, so continued to blame myself. This is when my body started to attack itself just has I had been doing to myself. I then understood I had to grow up and take responsibility, and because I felt it was my own fault, I realised I could learn from the experience and change everything in my life. I began to feel like I had control again, and it was *me* I had control over. I accepted that my connections to my destructive thoughts on health were not helping but making things worse, so I replaced them with thoughts of what I desired.

With all my body complications, my determination and desire to heal was extremely strong so this was the perfect time to take more control of my state of thinking. I started focusing on changing my belief systems about myself in all areas and especially my health. My old negative thinking continued to return with all the reasons why I could not be healed. This way of thinking has never got me anywhere good, it only lead to more health problems, so I continued to replace those destructive thoughts and saw in my mind only that my body was whole, healthy, complete and functioned in perfect balance and harmony. Because I desired so much to be healthy again I automatically took responsibility and action to find expert health advice, and I did everything I could to heal. I also accepted that my insecurities were also causing a victim consciousness. I began to change how I was thinking about everything and decided I was going to change my life.

What brought me to this new way of thinking was the spiritual connection I allowed myself to reconnect with. After all my prayers and connecting with the divine energy, I began to find answers for healing myself.. I wanted to feel happy again and have purpose. My 'knowing' as a young child came flooding back, as if I had buried this child's thoughts a long time ago. I then realised in this moment that life and everyone in my life had conditioned my way of thinking. I had allowed my mind to be consumed with the negativity I saw in the world. Because I wanted to change people's lives so much, I began focusing on what was wrong with everyone and everything, and then I unconsciously became conditioned with destructive thinking. Not only did I have dysfunctional emotions about myself but I created more over time.

After my new profound experience in myself I had moved into new beginnings, and the things that were challenging me at that time gave me the perfect opportunity to make some new decisions. I still kept following my direction but this time knowing what felt best for me. If it meant I needed to go one direction in life to learn something, then so be it. I knew I had to learn and grow to make change.

When I began seeing my life in this way I began automatically feeling stronger and detached from the outcomes. I began observing my circumstances and seeing them for how I had created and allowed a certain experience to unfold and how I began taking back control in a situation where I was not feeling fulfilled. It didn't happen overnight but at least I took responsibility and took action to begin making changes. I had been living a life as a victim, and I no longer wanted to be in this place. I realised it was up to me to change, and to change how I thought and learn from experience.

Since then I have focused more consciously on my direction in life – and the creativity, wisdom, spiritual connection, healing abilities and love for my worth, and I now realise I have been blessed with ideas to help humanity.

The ideas that have come through my higher self are perfect creations that will help a lot of people. It is up to me to bring these ideas into our physical world. As a child, all along I wanted to do great things, and it was my lessons and experience in life that have helped me to have compassion for others without judging them, but instead identifying the areas in which others can change. I am still on a great journey and will always be, as I never stop growing. I am now seeing positive life changes because of the experience I have had and the growth I am continuing to go through. I would not change anything because I have become so much stronger. I have stayed true to my authentic self, and my mission in life is to help anybody in need to change their destructive world.

I have gone through huge transformations in my life and in the past had so much continuous drama because of my destructive thinking, but my persistence has pulled me through because a part of me knew I deserved better and even more so that my DESIRE to impact others is the most important part of the equation. Desire is everything – it is what makes us move through obstacles and achieve the results we long for. When we are dissatisfied with life we desire change, and this is what fuels our motives and decisions.

You are worth so much more than you realise, you are gifted in so many ways, and those gifts can also help other people change their lives. When you know your worth you will make a clear decision to live your life with worthy purpose.

Today I understand and implement this NEW AWARENESS of my worthy purpose as a spiritual being, *which I KNOW I am*. I am directly connected to spirit, and spirit flows to and through me as I am one and the same. I will always bring about what I think about, therefore I commit to thinking of only what I desire. I am so much more aware of myself and the power of my mind. Every day I continue to grow and stretch my awareness. When this happens, better and bigger opportunities come into my life.

Now it is your turn to begin this journey.

This is the real beginning
of the life YOU were meant to live
along with the miracles YOU are about to experience.

All because YOU are
CHOOSING TO CHANGE.

You are about to really discover the
POWER OF YOUR DESIRE AND YOUR MIND
and transform your life
so you can now live
your
LIFE'S PURPOSE.

Chapter One

Introduction

We all have a desire to do something wonderful with our lives in whatever form we may imagine, and sometimes life does not go how we think it should. Let's just say most of us feel life doesn't go our way.

From the start maybe we didn't have a plan, or we though we didn't learn enough in school, or we were not talented enough like our friend or our brother or sister. Maybe we are just too shy and guessed no one would listen to us. We felt inferior because we never got supported like so-in-so was, or we were told we were worthless or always compared to others, which destroyed what little confidence we had left. We may have been bullied at school and then became a victim to others. When you get bullied you feel hurt, alone, afraid and most of all unloved and not accepted. This alone can make you feel you don't deserve any better – and worse, don't belong in this world. This is far from the truth of your existence.

Each person on this planet has the right to be here and to experience ultimate happiness, wealth, health, abundance and most of all, love. If you have experienced any hardship in your life, in whatever form, you may have been or are still going through challenges, then be assured that you certainly do have a particular special purpose in your life. I say this because most people who experience hard times can always use that experience to help others and be a role model for change. Life is to undergo growth, and the only way to do this is to learn from what went wrong, or is wrong, or how we created a life of struggle. Experience is the most valuable thing you hold, and no one has ever experienced things in the same way you have. Therefore you have a story to tell.

When you learn more about the importance of your existence you will come to understand how valuable your part in the world is. You are not only just living, you are here for a specific reason. You may or may not believe it but that doesn't change this truth. Things don't just appear for nothing, there is always a connection to everything and a reason for choice and for expansion. The only thing you are responsible for is to live the life you were born to live. Have you ever heard about your 'Life's Blueprint'? This is exactly what each of us has been blessed with. Why? Well, you will learn more about the essence of your existence as you read on further.

Firstly I want to talk more about what is happening on a day-to-day basis with most people functioning in this world. And the worst part is the fact that we allow ourselves to have no control over our destiny, and don't shape our lives exactly how we desire. I am going to be blunt with you and spell it out. You are failing yourself only because you have not taken the time to discover more about yourself up until now. What you are about to read and discover will truly change your life for good. Once you know this information about yourself you will never return to that lack of awareness in this area again – unless you deny your own power, that is.

The Mind

The mind is the key to something magnificent. You may have heard that we only use a certain percentage of our mind's capacity. It is true, but how much can never be measured because our mind is complex – it is an infinite tool of expansion that cannot be measured by the mind itself due to the fact that our awareness keeps on expanding. So once we are aware to a certain degree then we may think 'that is it'; however, that is never it, as there is always more to learn. It is never-ending. For example, it is knowing that you know something and knowing that you know that something.

The best way I can put it in simpler terms is to compare us to something else living which also has an intellectual mind. For instance, animals have a mind but their awareness capacity is much lower than the human's mind. We have learnt to physically move, read, write and think, whereas an animal follows its movements by reaction. What I am saying is an animal cannot decide that they will act according to what chaos is around them. What happens is that they will react to their surroundings to the extent that their awareness level makes them react to their need for survival. We can tend to do the same

A dog can be a man's best friend because of his intelligence. Humans have the ability to respond intelligently if they so choose. To adapt a habit of responding rather than reacting, we must learn to think.

This is something you can practise every day until you get into an automatic habit. When someone ruffles your feathers, instead of doing your natural reactive habit, begin thinking about how you will respond to their actions or words. This will help you feel in control of yourself and the situation. You will not only become clear in your thinking, you will create a positive outcome for the situation at hand.

As humans we are a very gifted species as we have a natural intellect that we use every day to make decisions for whatever we may desire. However, some of these decisions can be made from fear, self-doubt, habit, lack of confidence, confusion and comparison to others, and so on. If you really take a look at how you make decisions and the reason why, then you will find this interesting in itself.

Because we have an ability to think and make decisions, we can change our world accordingly. And there is much more to this than just thinking and making decisions to free up our life. It works on a higher level than just in our minds. Let's start with understanding things in a better order, which may reveal some truths about your existence.

There are thousands of reasons going around in our minds of why we cannot do something to better ourselves and better our lives. My book and Workbook will give you more than just hope; they will give you the freedom to live the life you desire. I am solely writing my story, my experiences and the truth of our Universal Power to give you a new way of living. My desire is to inspire others to be free to live the blueprint of their life and, most of all, be free in their heart.

I am a perfect example of someone who wants to change their life and do great things in the world. I am a big dreamer. But I have lacked so much more I didn't know I lacked. There is no point just dreaming big if you don't put ideas into action, and that is exactly what I have lacked. I have always been aware that I have consciously been connected to my higher self, but the self-destructive thoughts I had about myself kept me stuck and victimised. I used to get so frustrated with life, and most of all I used to blame others for my circumstances. I would expect others to be true to me, support me, encourage me and help me in my goals. Why did I think this? Well, there are many reasons but two that stand out – one, because I didn't know how to make things happen and always thought I had to be in a positive position before taking action and conditioned to never taking risks and playing it safe, even though I knew risk-taking was essential; the second reason is because I did not know people would listen to what I had to say, and this belief merely came from my early childhood conditioning.

However, from my experience, people are all ears when it comes to what I have overcome but only if they are ready to make change. So of course people want to hear how others have suffered and come out on top. I clearly remember telling people how they should change when they didn't have any desire to change. So in that sense, who on earth is going to listen to someone when they don't want to make changes? This is how I conditioned myself, thinking others wouldn't listen to me, when it had nothing to do with me but everything to do with their choice.

I learnt from relationships, jobs, friends, loved ones and all the immature decisions I made. The biggest thing I learnt from all the decisions and my experiences is that it had nothing to do with any of these people or situations. Everything I created in relationships, jobs, friends and so on, was simply how I thought about myself. You may not like me saying this, but believe me, it has everything to do with your self-destructive thoughts about yourself. These thoughts are most likely not conscious, they are embedded in your subconscious mind. As you read you will understand more of what I mean. You see, part of me knew my abilities, yet I could not see past the struggle. I knew I had big dreams, and I wanted to fulfil them. I didn't want to stay just a dreamer, so I decided to put my dreams into action and bring them into reality. This is what I have lacked for many years – putting my knowledge into action. It is because of how I was wired and how I had been conditioned by the outside world. And with the ultimate knowledge I have now learnt about myself and now experienced, there is no doubt my dreams are most definitely always coming true.

Most of us don't really have a plan, and if we do, then the plan doesn't seem to work how we thought. No matter how much you want it, the wrong outcome keeps occurring in every direction you turn.

Well the good news is that it only comes down to unconscious programming. You can truly change your life just by the knowledge you will read in my book. It is a Little Life's Handbook – how to find your purpose and live your life's desire as it relates to every situation you have ever experienced and any difficult future experiences you may come across. When we learn to use our ability to perceive opportunities in life and challenges we are going through, we begin to change our consciousness and this will determine our future reality. There is so much more to life than we realise. Our infinite power is incredible, and if we just allow our direct link with our own soul and our true purpose, we can create a life of miracles.

> *To start this journey of self-discovery is an incredible, exciting journey.*

Now, let's say if we were, just for a moment, able to wave a magic wand and change our life challenges which we are experiencing in our life today, how much better would we feel? Would we feel so happy and so abundant in having all we desire? Would we feel like we had made it to where we wanted to be? Would we be happy with someone we found for a lifelong partner?

I would imagine you, of course, would be saying right now: 'Yes, this would work great for me'. What if I told you that you actually, truly have your own potential to get exactly what you DESIRE in your life?

> You DO have the power to change your life and exactly how you DESIRE it to be.

We live for DESIRE. Everything you do relates to what you want to achieve. Even the smallest things in life. The purpose of every choice you make is associated with you wanting something from what you decide to do.

Now, keeping your mind open while I explain further, do you really believe all your problems would disappear if you started working on your dreams and following your heart's desires? Yes, to some extent they would. However, you would still most likely desire more. I don't mean to burst your perfect little bubble of the vision you keep in your mind for where you want to be. I just want you to realise the human self never stops wanting. Don't get me wrong, this is a healthy condition. Desire is what fuels us and expands our conscious awareness. By conscious awareness I mean the mental faculties you use every day, which is the power of your thought and the effect it has on your life. You of course will feel happier working towards your true goals to achieve everything your heart desires, but your negative thoughts can still come to the surface as you test your potential. This is where the challenge really begins.

We should strive to be happy, although to stay dissatisfied is a healthy state of mind. So rather than living in the comfort of no growth but still receiving the same things you *don't* want in life, you will be moving towards the new life you *do* desire, because you are dissatisfied. If this does not make sense, then see it this way You are happy, positive and grateful every day for what you already have in your life, but you desire to achieve larger goals – this is what keeps you moving forward to further expand your awareness and potential of who you truly are. Now if you did not have dissatisfaction, you would have no reason to strive forward, as you would have no reason to set goals. This eventually turns into feeling not so happy after a period of time. So setting goals is a natural habitual state to acquire.

We have over time learnt a lot of different ways about believing in your dreams, believing in your goals and focusing on your destination. I am not saying that none of this is good to do – it is very much something we need to do – but first **you need to have the foundation of abundance and the foundation of your existence**.

The foundation of abundance is living and breathing in a state of GRATITUDE for everything you have in your life today. The foundation of your existence is everything you DESIRE and the PURPOSE of your life. If you do not have this you will most likely never feel fulfilled and never seem to magnetise your true destiny. Just like building a house, you need the foundation first. You could be thinking 'how can I feel fulfilled when I am dissatisfied with my life?' Well, just because you are dissatisfied does not mean you are not fulfilled. Fulfilment is merely a state of productive achievement. When you move forward in taking action on your goals you will feel fulfilled doing so. So this helps you feel happy and fulfilled every day, knowing that you are living and moving on your pathway and your ultimate purpose.

You don't have to have reached a destination to feel fulfilled. But just by making a difference to your own life and to others, you will experience this feeling. But when you do attain a huge goal you will feel the emotion of achievement and proud of what you have accomplished. This is the icing on the cake, and it is part of your journey to multiply this feeling. So you will automatically create new goals. It becomes a wonderful, continuous fulfilling cycle of accomplishments. This is what life is all about. Expansion! And it is desire that motivates any person to grow.

So you need to understand how your mind works and the TRUE POTENTIAL of how it can create your outside world of what you want to experience. Your mind has an unlimited ability as it is directly connected to a creative, unseen energy force more powerful than you realise.

If you don't feel like you have anything good in your life, of course every day you are going to wake up seeing everything bad. This is obviously not a great start to the day.

Universal Laws

Throughout this book I will cover areas such as the Universal Laws (or Laws of the Universe) and how they are directly connected with our thoughts, emotions and actions, and how we automatically function on a daily basis, and then share with you the steps to change this through the daily process section.

There are many different Universal Laws; however, throughout the book I will mention some that are relevant to what I am explaining at the time.

By the end you will find you understand the essential Universal Principles and the power of your mind and emotions to create your desired reality. You will then be ready to put your knowing and understanding into action.

I will be giving you a free 40-page exercise Workbook that provides questions and steps to take, and is categorised into a specific order so you can answer all the questions in the correct order. Doing things in a precise order makes a huge difference to achieving progressive results. The universe functions in an orderly way, and when we align with order our world changes before our eyes.

I am not going to dwell on or discuss in depth too much your past experiences as you are only going to identify them so you can move forward positively. If you continue to function the way you are functioning today, you will probably never achieve your goals of happiness. Here are a few reasons why.

Whatever difficult experience you have had is clearly physically not happening now, except it is still having an undesired effect on your life. And let's bear in mind we are who we are today because of previous experiences. Our challenges make us stronger and able to find the core of our truth. They also allow us to dig deep into our hearts to find our true meaning in our lives.

The most important part of this process is the 'now' moment. This is the only place we can really change our conscious beliefs and subconscious conditioning.

> *Subconscious conditioning is an unknown conditioning we have collected from our past.*

You may have heard of neurological associations. This just means your brain has adopted paradigms. Of course there is more to neurological conditioning; however, I am keeping the explanation simple as I am not about to discuss the right and left brain functions – it is more about how and what we believe in our minds.

It is also about learning about how we 'train to believe' and then this belief creates circumstances that bring our desires into reality. What I mean by training to believe is what you form as paradigms. Paradigms are beliefs that have formed in your mind, and where you continue to create similar thoughts and actions because of these habitual beliefs. They are the same things as neurological associations or subconscious conditioning. Why I am explaining these terms very simply is so you can identify that we are talking about the same thing. If you have been reading anything about neurological associations then you will be able to adopt the same meaning to what I am explaining. Simply put, neurological association means that your mind associates circumstance with how society and negative life experiences have conditioned your mind. And this is exactly what subconscious conditioning is also about. It is through the subconscious that you can create new paradigms. Paradigms are what create the life you currently live.

> *When you are not willing to see how your paradigms are affecting your life, you lose the awareness of knowing how to change your life.*

If you want to change your life you have to change your paradigms. You will behave and think a certain way because you have been trained, or trained yourself, to think this way. A paradigm is the programing in your subconscious mind, done mostly by other people's habits. These habits have been passed down from generations and also from society and everything we have been exposed to as a child, and as we grow we continue to believe things that are destructive to living out our potential. Fear is a very powerful emotion, and this fear is what has been conditioned into many of us from our parents, friends, society, media and so on. We have been programmed unknowingly, and this is what is most destructive. The more dysfunction and destruction we see in the world, the more we are programmed to live a life of dysfunction and destruction. When we are unaware of what has happened to us, we cannot make change, but when we become aware of how we can make change, then we have the power to change and experience a brand new life.

The brain, as I have said, is very complex but our most valuable asset is our thinking ability and how we can take control of it. The best news is that we can actually reverse any negative conditioning – and it is easier than you think. You are absolutely right when you think it is hard to change something, because when you *think* something is hard, then it will *be* hard. Now if you think something is easy, you will train yourself to believe it is easy and your brain will work out all the reasons and ways of doing something to make it easier. This is what is so incredible about you – you are wired to work out any challenged situation so you can achieve something you strongly desire.

We all have a subconscious mind, and this mind is mostly what we are *not* aware of, and the messages we are receiving through the subconscious are what is so important to changing our life. There is a very easy way to identify these unspoken messages even if we don't consciously hear them playing at any given moment. I will refer to the subconscious mind throughout my book, as this is the ultimate power for change.

Anytime you are going through the exercise steps in the Workbook you will find you will have negative thoughts and emotions of the past, or what you think of yourself, or maybe even what someone else's opinion of you may be, coming to your mind. You will find throughout your normal functioning days, certain events will trigger these thoughts and emotions. This is all very normal, as the universe has a way of showing you what is locked into your subconscious. Now if you don't understand this just keep reading and it will make more sense.

> *The emotional reaction you get is the key to being aware of exactly what you need to heal. The subconscious mind and the emotional mind are tightly woven as one.*

Did it ever occur to you why we were born with the ability to use our emotions? Emotions are one of the most powerful tools we have, along with the power of the mind, and together they work in perfect synchronicity to create the reality of what we see in our physical world. This is called the **Law of Vibration and Attraction.** Our physical world is formed by the creation of an unknown force, as some people may call it. How many times do you ask yourself why do certain things happen to us, or in the world? Well, this is where the order of the universe speaks, and this order is strictly made up of Universal Laws.

Laws of the Universe

There are many laws of the universe. One I have mentioned is called the **Law of Vibration and Attraction.** This law is everything that exists in our reality today. We have attracted it by using the vibration we are functioning on.

I will continue to briefly mention some of the laws throughout the book as this way it will be easier to understand them and how they are relevant to the situation I am describing at that point.

Let me explain a very simple, physical law that we experience on a daily basis in regards to our planet: the **Law of Gravity.** As you know, this means 'what goes up must come down'. It is simply how we are magnetised onto this earth. If we did not have this law we would float around in the ether and therefore be non-existent. The only reason we know this law is because we physically experience it from the moment we are born and then learn about what it is. We continue to teach our children about this law to keep them safe.

Some other laws are just as important; however, they are unseen and not given much thought, but they play just as significant a role as the law of gravity. Each law is as important as the next. Understanding their importance helps us to use them to create the life we want.

The universe is merely a sea of energy created in all forms. This is called the **Law of Oneness.** It is as simple as it says – everything in the universe is connected to everything else. Everything we believe in, think about, take action on, or speak about, affects the universe and the world around us. We are one and the same.

We have an incredible creation at our fingertips, and most of us are not even aware this power even exists within us. Because we are part of the Universal Energy, just as anything else is, we of course have a direct link to this energy. Put simply, 'we are one and the same energy, just in a different form.

There have been many scientific studies done on the human body and how each of our cells are made up of pure energy that is tightly connected as one. This of course is what creates our physical being. I am not going to explain this as it is a whole subject on its own, but instead I will explain how we have the ability to bring about what we desire through being one with the Universal Energy.

Now that it is clear we cannot be anything other than part of the universe, we realise we are made up of the same energy. So if we are made up of the same energy, we know we have this power within our cells. This power is our key to everything. All movement and how it creates cause and effect.

Everything has to be in balance for our world to function in the right state. For example, our weather patterns express sunshine, rain, storms, thunder. It is all part of balancing our world. The same goes for everything else that exists, including our own being, which must function in balance, therefore we require certain elements that we are made up of - our mental intellect, our physical body, our emotions and our spiritual connection. We are spiritual beings having a physical experience, and for us to have this experience we need to be able to attain connection to our spiritual source of existence. When we are aware of this existence we can live a more fulfilled and purposeful life. To create balance in anything there must be an opposite to anything that exists in life. To master your thoughts and emotions is a vital key to becoming 'in balance' and therefore creating harmony within yourself, which will create harmony and balance in your physical world.

Everything in our existence runs under the Universal Laws. People may call these laws spiritual laws or laws of nature. However, it does not matter what we call them as it will not change the truth of the fact that they are unchanging principles. These principles will never change as they are part of everything that exists and how everything exists. They are what rule the entire universe.

When we understand these laws we can begin to live from these truths on a daily basis and create harmony by using the laws to assist us to create and enhance balance and order. Not only do these laws create balance and order, but they have the ability to directly create whatever we desire mentally, emotionally, spiritually and physically.

When we understand the laws we can begin to learn how to work with them, thus creating a prosperous life. The most amazing part of this equation is the fact that life will begin to be effortless as we become aware how to apply these principles on a daily basis. As you get in harmony with the laws you begin to get in harmony with your true self, and then your whole life will change.

Everything vibrates, as everything is energy, and energy is always moving in and out of form. **Energy just is.** When you are feeling great, you are vibrating in a positive vibration. The universe will always respond to match this vibration and reveal a mirror image of this feeling. It is your strong desire that creates a strong vibration that resonates with the Universal Energy. Why? Because you are the same energy as the Universal Energy but in a different form. Thought and emotional forms, however, are unseen but on the same frequency as the image you see in your mind's eye. This energy is directly linked to the universe therefore bringing what you desire into the mirror image.

Vibration is a vital key to attracting what you want. Energy is moving at all times through you and around you. To reiterate, when you are feeling great you are vibrating in a positive vibration. The reality in your life that you see is the manifestation of the non-physical world.

What I mean by this is whatever you have repeatedly thought about or desired, you will create it in your physical world. You express energy, and this is what creates cause and effect – it is called the **Law of Cause and Effect.** A cause will create an effect, just as an effect will create a cause. Reaction or action creates cause and effect. However, negative reaction will create a negative cause and effect, and vice versa – taking positive action will create a positive cause and effect. Simply put, everything you do will create an effect. Everything happens according to law.

> *The only thing that stops your desired reality is YOU.*

Your job is to recognise these emotions and accept why you may feel this way, then you will be shown a way for you to release it and allow the opposite emotion. By doing this you are then going to create a new association to this emotion. Sounds simple? Yes and no. It will really depend on you and the way you understand your mind, how much you want to change and how much you believe in changing. Bear in mind, as I mentioned earlier, there is always an opposite to anything in life. This is called the **Law of Polarity** – for example, good or bad, hot or cool, sad or happy, positive or negative and so on.

Remember I said mastering your thoughts and emotions is a vital key to becoming in balance. When a person is emotional, they usually have ups and downs, and this is because they are not in control of their mind and emotions. Wouldn't it feel great to go through life feeling emotionally balanced and happy on a daily basis? Well you really can if you desire to. It is a natural flow that you will go up and down through life, and this is also part of a natural law we can work with. It is called the **Law of Rhythm.** This rhythm will always bring you to the opposite so if you feel down you know you will get to feeling happy again. However, the ultimate is to be in control of this balance so you can feel wonderful most of the time.

I can give you tools to create new habits to transform your thoughts and emotions every time you are met with challenges in life. If at all you feel you want to be part of a community or continuous knowledge that works with people to assist them making permanent change in their life, then you can find this support by going to my website (refer to the end of the book).

Transforming your thoughts while experiencing your challenges in doing so is all part of your journey to unlock the freedom of your heart. What is and what happens is all part of your growth, and our subconscious mind is always playing out in our life so we can recognise and heal these parts of ourselves. What I mean by 'the subconscious is playing out in our life' is that our subconscious is the same as the Universal Energy, as I have explained previously.

> *The subconscious mind is the interpreter between our physical world and the universal world.*

Both of these two worlds are at our feet so we have the power to create the universe, to magnetise our desires, if we understand how we can use the unlimited potential that lies within each of us.

We are the ones who can make this change, and you *must* use your inner powers with awareness or you will be used by them. Your current thoughts and emotions are unconsciously creating a world you do not want.

> You have two choices:
> reclaim your subconscious mind to your advantage and take your powers back or be stolen by them.

Everything you see in your world today is an expression of the unconscious messages playing out all the time. You must change these messages in order to change your reality.

By reclaiming back your subconscious mind, I mean taking back complete control over your thoughts.

This is the problem with having such strong powers locked up inside each of us but you can choose to consciously take control of these powers to your advantage.

As I said, there is an opposite to everything, so if you use positive thoughts instead of negative thoughts and emotions, you will recreate a healthy subconscious mind that is playing out what you want in life.

Once you actually make conscious decisions to create new paradigms, then you will see things change in your physical world.

Look around you and recognise everything you do not want and realise that all this will change now you have made a clear decision – you will begin to draw in people to assist you along the way, in whatever form that may take, and situations will continue to challenge you so you can gain further awareness in changing your thinking and habits to successfully break the recurring cycles.

It is not the challenges that come your way, but how you react to a situation, that will show your habitual behaviours; in other words we can recognise these behaviours by the challenges we are experiencing, and this becomes a measure of your conscious awareness and the growth you have achieved in yourself.

> *If you do not become consciously aware of something, how can you change it?*
> *It is that simple.*

This does not have to be a hard process for you; it depends on the level of resistance you have to change. The more you resist the more it persist.

The more you desire something, the more you can allow the process of growth to unfold, and take responsibility for your actions and choices, and the faster and more easily life aligns with your consciousness and subconscious.

You will notice a lot of changes, such as certain people and friends coming in and out of your life. You could notice career changes, as you may have altered your focus and now have begun a commitment to your passion in life.

To achieve these changes you also need to be conscious of modifying how you focus on a daily basis.

> Order of the mind is very important as it allows you to exercise self-control and to set clear goals.
> This will eliminate creating dysfunction, clutter, confusion and mental hurry.

So take note of all these things that may occur every day, and enjoy this journey to your new life.

Chapter Two

Thought Forms

Thought forms come from a lot of conditioning; they are generated from our past, our present, and our future.

When we create thought forms we also create emotion, which creates energy inside of us; this causes a reaction and we then play out this reaction into action.

Re-action creates action.

E-motion creates motion, and vice versa – motion creates emotion.

If you take action on something it makes you feel a certain way, so you can make yourself feel great just by taking action on something you have put off for a long time. This is another way we can choose our emotions.

If any of the above sounds confusing to you at this stage just read it a few more times till it is clear. We will cover this further on in the Workbook.

In life we are taught about things we can only physically see or have a scientific reason for, and there are three types of energies most of us understand in everyday life.

Kinetic energy refers to moving objects. So you can think of kinetic energy as the **energy of movement,** because it refers to any object moving at any particular time. It can be changed into other sorts of energy, such as heat, light, sound, or mechanical or electrical energy.

Potential energy is a form of stored energy. For example, when we carry a rock up a hill and leave it there, the rock gains gravitational potential energy. When we stretch a rubber band, we say it has gained elastic potential energy. Food we eat has chemical potential energy. Batteries also have chemical potential energy.

Static energy is a form of high-voltage energy. For example, suppose you rub a balloon on your arm. Hold it near your arm, and your hair stands up. You probably don't realise but it requires around 100,000 volts to make your arm hair rise like that.

Now the other energy I will describe is more unseen. This is an 'invisible' type of kinetic energy (energy of movement). However, some people can see it in their mind's eye and some not, but it does not mean it is not there just because it can't be seen. These forms are created in thought, emotions and action. A thought form is a manifestation of mental energy. Mental energy is carried by the ether, which the universe automatically responds to, as all energy is part of the universe. Ether is the same as Universal Energy.

Thinking is very powerful, and when we consciously think we can programme ourselves to whatever we wish to achieve. A thought form can then create an emotion. This emotion is used to react to any given situation. This situation you are experiencing is manifested from your subconscious and/or your conscious thoughts, which have been triggered from your subconscious, which in turn have been created from your past or your future.

Therefore, in simple words, *a thought form is its own energy in motion. Even though we cannot see this energy, it does not mean it does not exist and travel through the ether.*

We see light, but we don't see sound – we hear sound. We see physical ailments in the body but we don't see the pain – we feel pain. For us to tell if someone is in pain is to see their expression and to hear them cry from that pain.

Pain is energy in motion that is unseen, but it creates cause and effect. I am only telling what we already know happens on a daily basis; however, I am explaining it in detail to take it that one step further so you can understand how your own thoughts and emotions can create cause and effect. It comes down to having a good attitude.

It is wise to begin to look at your own attitude you choose to have every day, as this is a classic example of cause and effect. You alone can be creating dysfunction in your life by putting out negative vibes. **These vibes are in direct relationship with Universal Energy.** This energy is a negative vibration, unseen except in the physical form of emotion, body gestures and negative thoughts and speech.

The Law of Attraction, which in turn is the Universal Law, will mirror the energy you give out. As I said, cause and effect. The old saying goes: 'You reap what you sow.' It's true! This is a huge realisation for your current life situations and your future.

You are probably thinking, 'how can my thoughts create my future?' as you alone are not in control of the world. Well, you are not in control of anyone else's world, but you are certainly in control of yours. We will cover this a little later but for now we will discuss subconscious conditioning and how it affects us and how you can change your mindset and create your desired world.

> *Remember all thought forms are already a reality.*

If you have a desire or goal in mind, you have already created that goal or desire to be a physical reality in your future. Just because you don't experience it on a physical plane now does not mean it is not real. It *is* real because you had that thought and vision, and thought forms are a real energy, which come from the ether. The ether is, in other words, from the Universal Energy, which is directly your higher self.

The Power of Your Conscious and Subconscious Mind

So you are now aware that your subconscious conditioning/paradigms is a relationship you have with your thinking and your emotions. Your subconscious mind holds the answers to the reality of your life and what you physically experience. For example, if you have a fear of spiders, you have somewhere along the way automatically created a paradigm that you must fear spiders. If you have a repetitive negative situation from the past or through a particular point in your life where you experienced massive trauma, which you have never quite got over, you would find you make choices in life because of this negative association. This is the same as subconscious conditioning.

> This is where you can use your conscious mind
> to re-condition your subconscious mind.

Let me explain it in a way that may relate to you better.

Habitual behaviours have been programmed into us from the moment we were born. We have this programming everywhere around us – through our parents, society, media and so on. This conditioning begins to create belief systems to set a child up for life. The emotion around a child is extremely powerful, as emotion is what a newborn baby is sensitised to. At birth, a child's subconscious mind and emotional mind, as I said, is one and the same, and is completely open to receive whatever information is around, as their conscious mind has not yet been developed.

> The conscious mind has the ability to accept or reject
> an idea, an opinion and even an emotion.

However the subconscious mind does not have this ability. It will accept whatever it has been given because it is the direct link to the unseen energy that connects us to our infinite potential and power, the Universal Power.

A baby slowly learns its way of functioning as it grows. However, it is always going to grow with the programing it has been most influenced by. Therefore it begins from birth and whatever programming the baby is exposed to has been handed down from generation to generation.

As consciously aware adults, we are able to transform our negative habitual behaviours into positive habitual behaviours. The way we do this is to use our conscious mind to accept or reject whatever is going to move us in the direction of our ultimate dreams. This way we can change our outside world to whatever we desire it to be. If you don't understand yet you will, the more you read on.

When we are born we learn and grow from those who guide us on this journey. Some of us have brothers and sisters, and some don't. Again, they have an effect on the decisions we choose to make in life. We come into contact with so many different personalities and create relationships with people for whatever reason we feel at the time. These relationships, whether with family, friends, boyfriends, girlfriends, co-workers or teachers, all have an effect on the paradigms we form, therefore embedding negative habitual behaviours into our subconscious.

An example of how our mind can work and create havoc in our life is that sometimes our mind blocks out trauma; however, your subconscious mind will replay this negative message constantly because it does not have the ability to reject the incident due to the traumatic emotion that was involved, which in turn created the subconscious absorbing this memory and accepting the reality of it so rapidly. This negative message is playing endlessly, and you will find physical situations manifesting to you. You will probably have no conscious knowing of how and why such things are happening. I don't mean focus on the past – I am helping you to realise you have this association because of this incident that occurred in your life, or because of what you have always been told or heard as a child. Once you see this, you can make the connection to see it requires change. The old paradigm is not serving you at all; rather it is sabotaging your unique greatness. This is where we must acknowledge our negative conditioning that is playing out in our life.

> Our subconscious mind can be conditioned;
> in this way we can also reverse the negative conditioning
> into positive conditioning.
> So we can train our own mind to automate
> the messages we desire,
> which will change our life for good.

As mentioned before, our subconscious mind is the direct link to the Universal Energy; they are the same. Universal Energy determines the reality we see from the messages it receives from our subconscious mind. What I am saying is if you change your subconscious automated messages, then the Law of the Universe has to match these images/messages. Of course we are part of the universe, or we would not be here otherwise, therefore we have a subconscious mind, and this is where the magic of our life is created and brought into reality.

> The subconscious mind becomes an interpreter
> between the physical world and universal.

This is exactly how we have the potential to tap into our higher self, which is directly linked with the universal world. Now these changes of course don't happen at once as it takes time for our subconscious to believe in the new ideas – repetitive conditioning and continuous focus is the key to change. I will elaborate on this further throughout the book.

However when you begin to see these changes occurring in your life you then know you are reclaiming your subconscious mind. As I said earlier, this confirms that you are taking back complete control over your thoughts and that your subconscious mind is beginning to take these positive thoughts and integrate them as their new way of seeing the world. When the subconscious has achieved its new belief and vision then it can only do one thing – play out this reality into the physical world. It is that simple. When you can reclaim your thoughts, you reclaim your subconscious mind. What I mean by 'reclaiming' is when you get a negative, self-doubting, critical thought you immediately change that thought by replacing it with a new, encouraging, positive thought in relation to what you desire to have or be.

The first step is awareness. This relates to things we think, feel and act upon or what we don't act upon. Basically it is recognising our behaviour and motives on a daily basis. I suppose at this stage you may think that is overwhelming. Let me assure you it is not. All you are doing is being aware of yourself. If we don't know what is happening, how can we change something? The way we make this change is to understand that we are responsible for our own actions and the choices we have made and make constantly every day. We make these choices for whatever we *believe* will make us happy at the time, as happiness is truly what we desire.

Sometimes we make choices because we again BELIEVE we have no other choice. Notice I have emphasised the word 'believe'. Let's take believe as an example. Why do we believe in the first place? How did we even come to the realisation about what we believe? Who told us to believe in whatever we believe in? You might now be thinking why should you believe anything written in my book? Well, good question!

I can easily answer this. If you look around your life it may not be how you desire it to be. I know that because you are reading my book. First of all, if you were conditioned with the correct beliefs, wouldn't you have everything you desire in your life right now? Why is it we learn from those whose don't know how to make their lives better, yet they are sure they have taught you all you need to know to make *your* life just how you want it? By 'they' I mean not only parents, I am talking about any outside conditioning, such as society, media and people you have interacted with throughout your life.

How we form beliefs relates to the reason we have opinions and hold certain beliefs about life and ourselves – because of what we have learnt along the way and the relationships we have formed. Relationships are merely a vehicle to find the truth about who we really are. We will cover more on this topic in the relationship section further on, but for now, we have created beliefs and we need to know which ones are causing dysfunction in our lives and which are true to who we really are.

You are probably wondering how your beliefs, emotion and thoughts can affect your future, and how overwhelming it is to take on the responsibility to monitor yourself constantly, every day for the rest of your life. Well, the good news is your brain can learn to do this automatically, and you can make a choice to grow and change your dysfunction.

Once you are in control of your mind you do not have to monitor your thoughts the way you think you do. Your mind is extraordinarily powerful and very clever. If you train your mind with discipline, you will automatically reprogramme your old paradigms. It is not as hard as you think.

As an adult we become responsible for all we do and cannot blame anyone else for our experience. The not-so-good news some of you may find difficult to accept is that you must be completely honest with yourself about your fears, emotions and reason for choices you have made that have put you in your current situation. If you can do this you are ready for change and thus your life *can* change.

First of all we must understand why we need to be completely honest with ourselves. You are obviously a person who is searching for something better in life, and as I have mentioned earlier, you have chosen to change what you are now experiencing day-to-day. The desperation to avoid all these horrible situations we find we are experiencing in the moment is very simply explained, and believe me, you can profoundly change it with a few simple steps, which will make you feel great every day. I can easily assist you to create simple things, such as a 'Vision Board'; however, this is not going to fix your daily problems entirely just at this stage until you have your mindset on the right path.

I am firstly going to invite you to change your current situation right now. If you do this, when you do your vision board and goals, you will manifest into your life's real desires without desperation from fear. This is a vital key. By the way, don't underestimate the 'Vision Board'. It is a more powerful tool than you realise. Read on for the key to changing now.

> *The level of awareness*
> *will always validate a person's reasoning;*
> *therefore the mind will perceive*
> *what it is conditioned to believe.*

Chapter Three

Live In The Moment

Have you heard the expression 'live in the moment'? How many people today actually do this? I can say most people do not. The image that may pop in your mind might be of a monk who lives in a meditative state experiencing every moment of his day. I am not telling you that you need to learn to be a monk and practise meditating – even though monks have a blissful life, which is what they desire, but this obviously is not for you. However, I am going to share how meditation can be used throughout your day, anywhere, and how you can use it in a quick, easy step. I will explain to you how we function so much in a world of time and how our lives revolve around the clock. Also I am going to go one step further and explain about what you dis-like in your life and how you can instantly change your old habitual conditioning and anchor your emotions into the 'now moment' to manifest your desires.

Firstly we find we wake in the morning to be hit with the same reality. All some of us want to do is go back to sleep to avoid our day of issues we have created while trying to move forward to fashion the life we have in our perfect bubble. And to avoid going to work so we can pay the bills! Sounds like a mouthful to me, and this is exactly how overwhelmed most people feel. No matter how much we *don't* want to live this way, we feel there is no other choice about how we live and function on a daily basis to get the things we want. We realise things don't make sense – some people do well but others, no matter how hard they try, continue to struggle in reaching their goals.

What if I told you that you were taught wrongly?

> *You never have to, or had to, do anything you don't desire to do, to create what you want.*

Now how crazy does that sound. Well, you are living this way every day just because you were taught to. We are not crazy, we are just doing crazy things. Our parents are not crazy – they were taught the same way. Our world is designed to believe this is the way to move forward, when in fact it is not the way at all. It is so far from our reality to living our true, abundant life on all levels of our existence. However, in saying this, it still does not blame the conditions you have had to deal with, or the way we learn and grow in our lives. The reason for your existence and your chosen path is the fact you came into this life with everything around you being perfect for what you needed to learn to expand your conscious awareness and to evolve your soul. This is our soul's chosen journey.

When you were born you had to discover your physical abilities and the simple ways your body functions. We learnt about reading and writing and discovering the things we enjoyed. But along the way in other parts of our existence we were unconsciously being conditioned by our outside world – the relationships we were in, the media and society's beliefs. We began to compare ourselves with others and listen to others about how we should be and what we should be doing. We conditioned ourselves to believe this was the right way just because we were told by people who were also conditioned in the same way.

Generations have lived in victim consciousness for years, and now it is time, 'in this moment', for things to change. In the past ten years there has been enormous growth in our planet's consciousness. And just in the last couple of years the planet's energy shift has been even greater. This shift is speeding up constantly so our consciousness on the whole can move forward. We are progressing to a higher vibration of evolvement; whether you are conscious of this or not, it is still happening. If you become conscious of it, life will become easier as you understand the process. If you are not conscious of it, then life will become not as joyful, as you begin to feel like you are the victim and life is pushing you around.

One of the quickest ways to move forward for your own growth is to live your life in the moment as much as possible. Now I am not saying you walk around with your head in the clouds without any focus on the future. In life, focus is exactly what you do need; we came into this world with dreams and goals - this is exactly how we have grown and learn to achieve and move forward.

If you live in your past or in your future you are constantly avoiding the here and now. When you avoid the now, you are avoiding evolving. Also, you miss the chance to create your future in the here and now, through your subconscious mind, for your future reality.

Doesn't this sound confusing and contradictory? Let me explain further. The reason you may avoid the here and now could be, or is, the fact you do not want to address daily tasks and challenges and most of all your own insecurities.

Have you heard of people who strive ahead, focusing on being financially wealthy and having the best of everything at their feet. They achieve their desired dreams to be rich and when they reach this so-called place of freedom, they come to a realisation that they are not as content and happy as they thought they would be. They have all the money and nice things but they have destroyed relationships or marriage, have not found their lifelong partner, have lost close connections with family and friends or they find all the people who really mattered in their life just don't fit into theirs any longer.

> *Therefore*
> *it is not about the money ...*
> *it is all about DESIRE!*

There are so many negatives to the life they have created but they thought they were creating a life of freedom and happiness. Where did they go wrong? Maybe they made their money by violating the rights of others. These people exist all over our planet, trying to search for happiness. They always think money is the answer to their problems. I am not being judgmental, I am merely stating how some people believe they can find happiness.

Money is just a wonderful vehicle to learn about how we live, how we act and how we treat others, and what we would do for it. We place so much power in money and believe it will make us happy. It will buy us nice things and assist us to achieve our heartfelt dreams but definitely, money alone will not make us happy. Love is what it is all really about, and by that I mean self-love and to love others unconditionally. We place money in our world and strive only to achieve these riches just to cover up the true key to our happiness. We think money will solve everything but it is only one part of the equation. Don't get me wrong, money is to be desired without feeling guilty. All I am saying is find the happiness of your true desires and what your magnificent true self was born to do. Money is not a bad thing, it is a wonderful tool to live in comfort and help others enjoy all the best things in life, as we deserve abundance. Just keep in mind the reason you are striving for money, and is it going to be used in the highest form for yourself and humanity?

> *Money only becomes negative with the power we give it and how we use it.*

Our mind creates the dysfunction. It is about balance, and this balance comes from your inner balance.

To truly be free we must recognise our imbalances within and change what we must to find happiness on all levels of our existence.

When we sit quietly with ourselves and truly begin to be completely honest about what and why we have what we do in our life, we will find one answer, which most of us don't want to know.

'We are responsible.'

We are so busy blaming others and the outside world that we cannot even begin to look at ourselves. It is too easy to avoid our own actions and blame others. It is not just why we do it; it is because this is the pattern we have learnt and been conditioned from generations before us. The moment is now, which we can change. We are responsible because we are now adults and have no excuse to complain or blame anyone else or anything else for our own emotional dysfunction.

We may think we know how to make choices in life yet we find that the choices we made have caused us more grief, but they are our own, for which we are responsible. No one forces us to do anything – it is ultimately us who make the choice in the end. If we choose to stay in victim consciousness, we choose to live a life of misery.

If you continue to function with dysfunction, you will most likely never achieve true happiness. There will be questions in the Workbook relating to the victim roles you play in life so you can change and eliminate a lot of unnecessary heartache, pain and continuous health challenges.

TIME

Have you ever had thoughts about how you never feel you have enough time in the day to do all you want to? I'm sure we all feel this way at some point. If you really think about it, time does not truly exist. Of course you would say this is impossible to believe as we function by the clock every day. So let me explain.

Time is a form of measurement that exists only in our physical world and assists in helping humanity function in synchronicity. It is a measure of past, present and future. These are bodies of experience that are forever changing based on the passage of time. The only reason they change is because we function in a physical world of which time also has a physical energy. The energy of time is to continually move forward, and this is what creates our past, present and future. They are separated by seconds, minutes, hours, days, weeks, months and years. So time is put into units of measurement to create the passage of time.

Long ago time was easily created from the synchronicity of the natural state in which day begins and night falls. This is the natural rotation of our earth on its axis and the revolution of the earth around the sun and the moon. These simple occurrences are what gave us our basic measurement of time. It was quite simply discovered that we assigned an unseen movement, which took us from one moment to the next, and eventually put it on a mechanical device we could physically see, to measure the time between sunrise and sunset. This turned out to be 24 hours. This discovery came from the creation of the universe. Everything created on the physical level was already created in the ether, the space that exists in the universe. This space is the creation that gets transferred through our subconscious mind, and with these creative ideas we had, and still have, the ability to bring them into physical reality just as they were meant to be. The universe will create and move towards your creation, as they are one and the same, and it wants to express itself only through you. Time is part of our physical world just as everything in the universe has its place of purpose in an orderly way.

If we had never invented time, what do you think would have happened to our world and where would it be? Now this is an interesting subject. I am sure you would think the world would be in chaos.

Well, let's look at another scenario. Just imagine how we would function without time. If we were all born with no ability to use time to measure our days, we would all function on an inner clock, in other words, our intuitive synchronicity with the Universal Energy. We would rise when the sun rises and go to sleep when night falls. If you can imagine this and apply this to your daily life, how would you function? I would say you would function very differently and there would be less pressure and stress in your life because you are not measuring your daily progress. In saying this, there is nothing wrong with pressure and stress in order to function in synergy, but I am merely making a point of how different we would operate in our daily tasks. Maybe if we were born into a world without time, we would all automatically be in sync with the planet as a whole, and our level of intuition would be so powerful that our world would function around us completely differently from how it does today. Synchronicity of our moments may likely align perfectly without any force or planning. All would be as it should in any given moment, and we as individuals would not have learnt what resistance is. If every single person on the planet were in sync intuitively, maybe our world would be so connected that our planet would not be as it is today. In saying this, our world is perfect just as it is, and as it was created, therefore time was meant to be part of our physical existence.

There is a reason for everything so remember the universe created time for a purpose, and for us to use time to be in sync, as that is how we can determine synchronicity, by something physical. So the human reality of being in sync without time would not be suited for growth in the human race. We need to use resistance to measure progress in moving forward. It is all part of exactly where we need to be and how we need to experience and learn.

Part of this learning is to discover and develop our intuition for functioning in a world that operates in the synchronicity of time. The more we practise using our intuition, the stronger it becomes. And why? Because it is a natural ability we have, but some of us have allowed this ability to be unused since birth. So when you use repetition and practise something new, this begins to be a familiar action, and thus our intuition becomes an automatic response.

From the beginning of time, the reason why man was endowed with the time factor was to bring in the creation of measuring humanity's synchronicity, because the soul does not relate to time. Our souls came to be here, wanting to experience a physical body and to function in a world of time, and to allow the denser energy of the physical plane to work in sync, and by having the experience to learn who we are on all levels.

We need to go one step further to understand how we are connected strongly with time and how we can change time. This may sound bizzare but let me explain. How many times have you heard people say 'time is speeding up', 'time goes by so fast', 'there never seems to be enough time in the day these days'? Most people agree it is because we are getting busy with our lives and time goes by so quickly. Well, I see it a little differently. Open your mind for a moment and go back a little bit here. As I mentioned, our soul energy does not function on a time basis.

Spirit energy is 100% everywhere at exactly the same moment.

Our physical world measures by time; however, the Universal Energy does not, because it is the same everywhere in every moment. But in saying this, due to the fact that we use time as a measurement, then this is also part of the Universal Energy but on a different level. Spirit energy takes different forms; however, it is still everywhere in those different forms in that same moment. All I am saying is we have the power to use spirit energy to be where we want it to be and when. **Why do we have this**

power? Because we are that same energy, but in a different form. We are in the physical form of this radiating energy, and because we are one and the same we can move and shift this energy into any form we desire, through our subconscious mind. That is the direct link we have with the vibrating Universal Energy. How we use this energy is through our heart centre, and I will explain that further on.

Your Soul Essence

Each soul is born to learn to be in a world that functions opposite to the energy of the soul. We are spiritual beings having a physical experience. We come to be in this world to learn to function with our soul essence in a physical body, to learn more about experiencing our own soul energy. If this sounds confusing it might be because it is a new way for you to look at yourself. Let me explain another way. Imagine you have gone through a negative experience; you then come out of that negative experience and have a realisation and find yourself asking: 'why did I even go down that path?' Well the answer is you had to go down that path to learn for yourself so you can grow. It took that experience for you to learn what you were really doing and in the process find out who you really are. It is that simple.

The unknown force to which some of us would relate, such as energy, God, Universal Law, divine energy or whatever you wish to call it, created the perfect vehicle to learn who we truly are. To me they are all the same. When we really know the power we have of creation, we will never again question our experiences and why things happen to us.

Now, if your question is: 'how do we know we chose this experience here on earth?' Well the answer is very simple – you just know that you know that you know that you know … Your soul always knows. If we connect deeply to our own soul's essence we will find that knowing, and then we will know that we know that we know …

Nothing happens to us, it is from our creation to learn and evolve. This creation is the world we choose to live in and the world we created today. So if we exist here on this planet, then we are here to grow, and the world around us is a reflection of our beliefs and our existence to learn and remember who we already are and have already been.

If you find this is too hard to grasp, there is no need to worry about trying to get your head around it, as it doesn't matter, because as you go through your life's journey you grow, learn and therefore awaken, which always brings you back into the truth of your existence. Our soul already knows who it is; however, placing a soul into a human body completely changes the soul's natural experience into a chosen experience.

As I have said before, we are spiritual beings who have chosen to have a physical experience – and the soul knows this – but use the human mind to remember this is a different experience all together. I say 'remember' because our mind is directly linked to our soul knowing; therefore, when we become more in tune with it, we then begin to remember what we have always known unconsciously, yet we are now becoming consciously aware. In other words it is linking into what your soul already knows. Therefore we begin to see how we have this knowledge but we now realise that we know it comes from our higher self.

Knowing who we are, and what it is we desire to do on this planet, is the key to living the life we dream of. Our purpose is set out in stone, which you can say is the blueprint to your life; however, we must follow through with our desires so we can experience why our soul came into this physical existence.

Whatever you desire now in your life, you are here to change your life to bring your desire to reality. Remember, though, all thought forms are already a reality. All each of us really desires is to be truly happy. This is indeed the beginning of your awakened journey.

Chapter Four

Health, Consciousness and the Subconscious Mind

Emotions are an amazing tool for us to identify areas in need of healing, change and growth. Our emotions are very powerful, more than we think they are. They have a huge impact with our mind and body on a daily basis. You may be thinking how could I possibly have created this health issue with my emotions? I will cover a little on this topic so you have a clearer understanding.

Here's an insight into how our emotions affect the body.

> *When we hold unhealthy emotions in our body we hold dis-ease in our body.*

Let's separate the word for a moment – dis-ease. We are not at ease, we are in dis-ease. This is exactly the relationship our body has with our emotions. Our emotions have to go somewhere, and if we don't deal with and free them they then become locked in every cell of our body, which then creates dis-ease. Our body is magnificent, and how each cell holds on to this emotional energy creates a huge impact. As I told you before, we are here to grow and learn and to become aware of who we really are. So our emotions are a huge tool in showing us what we need to heal, to create the happy life we came here for. Because you did not become aware of what emotions you locked into your body and mind, your body has now manifested dis-ease and is now giving you the answer to heal your life and health problems that you experience to this day.

At the moment maybe you are thinking this is a load of hogwash and how can it be my fault. Let's take a weak back for example. We'll look at this problem for a moment. What is a weak back? Of course you would think the obvious and say, "I just have a weak back because of the accident", for instance. Yes, and such and such gave you this ongoing back strain; however, it has a deeper meaning than just the accident. The accident was a catalyst in playing out those locked-in emotions. Remember what we hold in our subconscious and the consciousness we create.

Just for a moment, look at it this way. Your back is the main structure of your body. It is your skeleton to hold up your body and creates support for the whole body to stay intact and to function with movement. If your back is misaligned and/or in pain, it does not do its job very well. In other words, it is not supporting your body the way it is supposed to. Now if we take for an example our emotions at this time, while experiencing our back problem, we could identify in our life, at the exact same time, that we were not supporting ourselves. If we ask this question about how we are lacking support, then we can find the link with our body and our emotions. We then begin to see the connection and the timing is definitely not a coincidence. Your subconscious mind plays out exactly what you keep telling it. It does not know any different to what you tell it. And your body is an instrument of subconscious conditioning. In other words, if you tell yourself in life that you are not supported financially, emotionally or whatever you believe is the case, of course your body would manifest being unsupported. For instance, the spine is what physically supports our entire body, so with the mind thinking unsupportive thoughts, naturally the spine would continue to have issues in supporting the body.

Taking responsibility for this awareness begins healing your body instantly as you become connected so much more with your emotional body/subconscious body, then you allow the healing process to begin. This is just the beginning of a healthier you. People have learnt it back to front.

People do what they think they must to survive.
To survive people avoid feeling.
To allow your feelings to be free
You allow your body to be alive.
And this is when you balance emotion
And where the healing begins
Therefore your essence becomes in sync
And your body allows energy to be free in motion.

For a more in-depth understanding I suggest you read the book called *You Can Heal Your Life* by Louise L Hay. (Please visit my website **www.1-desire.com** for a link to this book.)

It explains exactly which disease is created from which emotion. It is a must read and will change your concept on health and help you heal your body where it needs it. Once you can free your sabotaging emotions, you are ready to allow the replacement of good emotion therefore creating ease in your health rather than dis-ease. You will also find that you will make healthier eating choices, and this again is a new belief being conditioned into the subconscious mind. So whatever you are healing emotionally, your actions will automatically progress into a 'health conscience' as you make clear decisions to identify and cure all parts of your being. This will heal your subconscious conditioning, thereby creating the life you desire.

Healthy Boundaries

This might be a topic you may not have talked about before, or even given it a thought, as to how boundaries you place or don't place in your life have such a great effect on you and the challenges you face daily.

Boundaries are something that each person knows what is right for them in life. All we need to do as an individual is know ourselves and have respect for ourselves to implement certain boundaries. By doing this you can, by yourself, create a huge impact on your life in so many areas in need of change.

If we were to **love ourselves enough to respect ourselves enough** to set clear, healthy boundaries with all the relationships and communication we have every day, we would find others would have a great deal of respect for us. Not only would you gain respect, but life around you would change so dramatically, as in all areas in need of change, that you would begin to automatically place boundaries.

For an example, let's take a situation where people may have told you sometime in your life that you are being a doormat, so to speak. Of course you know what a doormat is. A doormat's job is to lie there in front of your door allowing whoever comes along to wipe their feet before entering your home. I have described it exactly like this because this is exactly what you are allowing yourself to become. A doormat person definitely does not have a lot of healthy boundaries – if any at all. If you feel this sounds a little like you, you can now recognise where you need to change your life and what you need to do. All humans would recognise that at some point in their life they have experienced being bullied, emotionally and mentally controlled, or abused. To have this experience is just a matter of recognising where you lack boundaries. Remember it is not about blaming others for treating you like a doormat; it is you who place those boundaries and allow others to do it to you. Remember, you are responsible.

Now one reason for not placing boundaries in your life is merely because you don't value yourself. You feel that to make yourself valuable to others you need to lay yourself out to them and please them, even if it is not being true to yourself. This is not loving yourself and not how we bring love into our lives.

I will give you another example. This is a situation you may find a little difficult to listen to. Say you are in a relationship where you find yourself always being the one who is trying to keep the peace by not rocking the boat, as you do not want to upset the other person for whatever fearful reasons and insecurities *you* hold. Well, by doing this you are denying yourself a voice – you, who has beliefs and opinions – and not only that, you deny yourself the right to express your feelings. When your feelings are not expressed you then create an emotional unbalance as well as health problems, which we have just discussed. By continuing this process you are clearly saying to yourself: 'I am not worthy of an opinion. I don't love and respect myself enough to put myself before others.' But I do not mean that in a negative way. Let's look at how we are taught in an emergency during an accident. We are trained to first look after our own well-being so we can be of assistance to others in need. If we begin to take steps in valuing ourselves, enough to place boundaries around us, we then become a role model for others to do the same.

This is vital information for parents. If you have young children who are out of control, it is clearly because you have a subconscious paradigm that needs to be addressed in order to make a change. If your children are still at an age where they are in your care and you are responsible for them, now is the time to really make some changes within yourself so you can help your children before they go out into the world and create a life of dysfunction.

It is not about blaming yourself and feeling bad because you feel you have harmed your children. No parents' intention is to harm their children, we all just want to protect and love them the best way we know how, in others words, how we have been taught ourselves. And society and the media also condition our children, so it does not always come from the home. But it is the home environment that can make the change.

Remember you have been conditioned in a certain way; however, it is your duty to recognise your dysfunction and take full responsibility to make the difference now for your children's future. We don't want to place any outside dysfunctional conditioning on our children, thereby continuing a never-ending negative cycle.

Remember how your children love to play; well, when they do this they are really learning about everything in their surroundings, so they need to touch, feel and experience. Through this playful state of being comes their creativity in those moments. All change happens in the 'now moment' and it is vital you know your children are 100% receptive to the environment they live in. When you communicate through loving Eyes of Awareness you are setting up a positive pathway, as best as you can, for your child to live an abundant, happy and fulfilled life.

It is critical to remember this next time you are having challenges with your children – guide them through loving Eyes of Awareness.

If you have ongoing challenges with your children's behaviour, something clearly needs to be changed. If they have left home, they are ready to make their own choices, and this is when they become a young adult and learn about life, just as you did. What you can do is only change yourself, and once you change, your outside circumstances also change. You can live an example by living your life with awareness and loving them without your own destructive needs. By destructive needs I am referring to placing your needs on others and expecting them to be and do what you want.

We are already a role model in our children's life – it is essential to become a good role model and to have healthy boundaries to guide your children on the right path for them, not for you.

We are not only talking about our children's lives, we are talking about how much of an impact what we do now can have on the lives of so many others in the future who interact with your children, and how the values and morals they learn and continue to learn from you can help influence and change our planet as a whole. All parents want is for their children to be happy.

Our world is how it is because of our conditioning. Most parents would agree that we are trying to protect our children from the world we live in today. In fact, we are merely saying we are trying to protect our children from poor conditioning.

As a parent, every day of our lives, what we most want for

our children is for them to be happy and to make sure they aren't screaming for something or playing up, and if they listen to what we tell them then they will be okay and happy. This is not correct, but it is what we believe. Why we believe it is because of our own conditioning. We have probably all heard it before: "If you kids listen to your mother and your father, you won't go wrong." It does not work this way. It is time parents really understood how children function.

All children need is to be loved and respected, and they are wiser than you give them credit for. If you want your children to love you, they already do, as children have no agenda in loving you – they are pure and innocent and already know how to love unconditionally. It is us as adults who place conditions on love and create dysfunction for our children. Why? Because of our own conditioning. Children simply reach out to you for understanding and wise guidance. However, in saying this, it is healthy for children to learn about their own emotions, making decisions and growing in this world. Each of us would have experienced hurtful feelings as a child. If you look at what has happened to you, you can identify that you have grown stronger or you have limited yourself from an experience. It does not mean you blame others for your experiences.

Life as we are growing up is normally to feel all emotions that humans experience, thus we are challenged continually. All I am expressing here is that as a parent you can guide your children to grow with their own awareness and do the best they can. Life will still challenge them at different points in their life. It is a natural transition to help a child grow into adulthood. In saying this, you as an adult can now choose to transition yourself from the child and allow those emotions and experiences to be of the past. (*Refer to the Workbook for this process.*)

If you want your children to respect you then you need to respect them as people with a voice. This does not mean you give them what they want in materialistic items; all you need to give them is your time, understanding and healthy boundaries, and all with the awareness of who you really are without your negative conditioning. By doing this you are guiding them to be who they truly are and continue to grow and shine as they would naturally do. Their true gifts can develop much more quickly in life if you support their true potential.

Some parents who were brought up in a strict environment will usually either bring up their children strictly also or they will go opposite and set no clear boundaries because of their own neurological association with their childhood. These areas are clearly both unbalanced and it is up to us as adults to first be aware of this and then take responsibility and change it. If the parent is already aware of this childhood conditioning they have had, they should be able to bring up their own children in a balanced, disciplined environment. But as I said, this is because they have chosen to become aware, and awareness is the key to everything.

Take a look at why you are reading my book. Most probably because you need to un-do your negative conditioning. Most of us will automatically say it is because our parents told us this or that. Well, if our parents had the knowledge to raise us allowing us to have a voice and guiding us with love and awareness of the higher self, then we would have a different life today. This is not entirely true. Life will always throw curved balls because we are here to grow. It is not about blaming parents, as all parents do the best they can, as generations before conditioned them the same way.

By the way, your parents always love you – all their agenda

was, and still is, is to love you. They wanted so much to make sure they taught you what they thought was right for you to be protected in life.

Each child comes into the world being raised by parents with negative conditioning.

> *The newborn looks at life through the eyes they are given.*
> *Adults feel it is their job to imprint ideas and lessons,*
> *so we show them how to see*
> *and then they forget who they really are,*
> *as they look through our eyes instead.*

I suggest reading this statement a few times until you really understand it. Children's innocence and knowing, how to value themselves, their desires, dreams, and goals was left abandoned as they learned the way of the dysfunctional, conditioned world and what their parents/friends/media/society suggested they be or do. So it is not individuals alone who assist in this dysfunction, it is everything in life that you experience yourself.

We need to re-condition ourselves. And why did we forget about our desires? Because we never thought we had a belief that we could be all what we wanted to be. We were simply conditioned by life.

The next time your child is screaming for something is probably because they don't believe they have been heard. It is not about the lollies they are screaming for. Children are screaming for loving, healthy, wise boundaries, for which you are responsible for guiding them with great awareness. You have grown and healed yourself from your past conditioning and therefore perceive things in a balanced way. Your own awareness has changed your life, and therefore your responsibility as a parent is to assist your children with this newfound awareness.

Children are in a state of expectancy from others and only think of themselves getting what they require. It does not at all mean they are consciously selfish, it merely means they cannot fend for themselves and are always reliant on adults to keep them safe, feed them and give them happiness.

You choose to be a parent, and the gift of being one is so magnificent that all parents need to cherish and have gratitude for such a beautiful opportunity to guide our world into peace. This sounds a big responsibility, but really that is what your contribution is to the world, as a parent – to raise your children with love and awareness. Easier said than done, because if you have issues within yourself, it is a real challenge not to allow those issues to affect how you bring up your children.

How many couples out there, who cannot have children and desire so much, instead have the opportunity to adopt and love a child without parents. They also have opportunities to work with children in the future, which can give them more of an impact on a larger scale.

I know I have elaborated on this a lot and have repeated my points, but I have a powerful point to make. I am emphasising this topic as it all starts from childhood and your conditioning, and the outcome of your life.

We are gifted with children and relationships to mould and polish our character and expand our awareness. If we really listen to the *innocent* things children say we will hear so many enlightened messages through their voice. We will learn a lot about ourselves and our actions. We just don't choose to listen because we believe we are wiser.

> Remember the wiser one is the one who is untouched,
> and this is the pureness of the newborn baby
> before we download our generations
> of dysfunctional conditioning.

You alone have the power to mould your magnificence, and to do this is to change now just by being aware and being that role model of awareness.

> Be the change and their magnificent light will emerge
> in front of your eyes.

If you desire to follow through to change your life for good and to understand your current situations and where you desire to be, please continue to Chapter Five.

Chapter Five

The Power of Desire, Imagination and Emotions

Desire is one of the most incredible gifts we have to achieve our goals. Without desire we would most likely have no goals.

Imagination is misunderstood. Along with emotions and visualising, it plays a special role in bringing our desires to reality.

We have always been told to stop daydreaming; however, this is a vital part of creating what we want in our reality. Daydreaming is visualising an image in your mind along with the emotion of your desire on the image you are imagining.

> *Imagination is more of a reality than what you can see with your eyes; it is the key to your life's purpose and all of your heart's desires.*

Now most people reading this would say this is not true – "What you see is your reality." Well yes, that is true – your reality is what you are seeing – but your subconscious mind holds the key to your reality, so in saying this, if you were to picture your desires all the time, you would impact onto your subconscious mind those images of what you are imagining. Your subconscious mind will then in turn bring this vibration of thinking in from the universe to match exactly those images and desires. YOUR IMAGINATION NOW BECOMES YOUR REALITY.

As you know from the previous chapters the power of the subconscious mind, this is elaborating a step further in how we harness this power and use it to create your desire.

The way we impact our subconscious is by repetition and through feeling the emotion of the desired results. The subconscious mind works in manifesting your desire if it believes it is already in possession of it. Your subconscious mind does not know the difference as to what you have in the physical or in the ether. It is the conscious mind that continually sends the message to the subconscious mind that you have not got what you want yet.

> *The trick to imprinting the belief and reclaiming your subconscious mind is not to allow outside circumstances to dictate your reality.*
>
> *Therefore the more repetition you do with emotion, the more you condition your subconscious mind and the faster you will find yourself automatically move into action to achieve your results.*

As I have explained already, the subconscious mind does not know the difference between the physical reality and the imagination. It is only picking up on the images the consciousness is experiencing. So if you were to use emotion along with visualising your desire this will become even more powerful, then the subconscious mind has no alternative but to accept the images it is receiving. The subconscious mind and the emotional body is one and the same. You have the emotional faculty to impact your subconscious mind so you can create your desired reality. The reason your subconscious accepts these images and desires is because emotion is the vehicle that aligns and is in sync with the subconscious mind. It is very easy to understand how we can create our world when we understand this simple knowledge.

What you are experiencing now is most likely what you don't want, because our minds will naturally associate with what we see around us and confirm to us what we are seeing. Therefore we believe what we are seeing. This is true and it is correct. However, the subconscious mind can be tricked in a positive way. We know we learn from images, but did you know you can learn from your imagination also? Your imagination is such an incredible gift that we hardly ever use as an adult.

Let's look at why we continue to create what we don't want. For a start, what we are seeing in our reality is affirming what we don't want. So of course we will continue to create what we don't want. When the subconscious mind is repetitively seeing the same image it is affirming what you have manifested, and this is why you believe in what you see. This is exactly how we continue to repeat the negative cycle. We become confused in our own environment of our dysfunctional reality.

Now the good news is we have the ability to reject and accept something. The way we have this ability is through our subconscious mind. So if we continue to affirm something opposite to what our eyes see, we can begin to believe in it. How this works is through our imagination. The imagination can see pictures, and the subconscious mind does not know the difference between pictures we see through the eyes or through the imagination. Why is this so, you may ask? Well, the subconscious mind is directly connected to the Universal/Spirit Energy, and this energy exists everywhere in any form. So the imagination is in a form of images through the mind. Therefore it is exactly the same energy we may see through our eyes.

However, what makes this reality different in our physical experience is our human belief; seeing it with our conscious mind makes us believe it is real because we can see, hear, feel and touch it.

Of course this is true but only on this level of physical existence in this moment. We have been taught to learn and function this way. The subconscious mind has no ability to reject anything; whatever you continue to impress upon it, it has to accept. This is the valuable key to manifesting your new reality. By limiting our awareness of our ultimate potential we create a life hardly lived.

> *You need to become aware of this ability if you want to take control of YOUR life and enjoy everything YOUR heart desires.*

When you find yourself desiring something more than you have in your reality, it means you are dissatisfied with your current situation. However, it is very important not to allow yourself to be unhappy in your current reality; you must be grateful for what you have in your life while still desiring your goals. To be dissatisfied is a healthy emotion, as it creates a platform to strive forward with a focus with purpose. Being unhappy is creating a depressive attitude where you lose gratefulness for all the good you *do* have in your life. So you always want to stay in a vibration of gratefulness. The universe will respond to this vibration; it is called the **Law of Gratitude**.

> *Gratefulness is a vital key in sustaining a higher vibration therefore attracting good things into your life.*

As you will already have learnt, the universe will match the vibration on which you emanate. So if you are feeling grateful for what you have in your life, you will attract more things to be grateful for. The subconscious mind recognises that it has plenty to be happy about.

To keep your subconscious absorbing wonderful desires, you are reprogramming your subconscious mind to all the goals you are striving for. When you continuously feel grateful for everything in your life, you will always attract only the same as you are putting out. And to be truly grateful, you must continuously show gratitude and list everyday things you are grateful for until you feel this gratitude in every part of your being. This alone will change your life because of the new vibration you attain.

This is how you also reverse negative emotions, as you will wire yourself up to feeling grateful for all you have, rather than feeling negative about what you don't have. When you focus on what you don't have, you will continue to attract the same reality. So changing your emotions is a vital key to creating the new desired reality.

> *The universe only responds to energy and can only attract like energy, therefore it is by law the universe will bring you more of what you radiate.*

The most important part of this reprogramming is the fact that you truly are grateful for the simple things in life, and this alone is a wonderful way to live every single day.

There are exercises to do in the Workbook that will help you change any negative emotions you have about anything.

As children we used to have such strong imaginations and as we got older we forgot how to dream about our desires. I suggest you start imagination exercises every day and never stop. Firstly you will discover what you truly desire, and anything you truly desire is what you are born to have. The most important thing to remember is to find that your desire is most likely something you don't believe you can achieve or even have the ability to do. But if it is a burning desire within you, you know it is your life's purpose and you were destined to do it. I suggest you never allow any outside opinions on what you should be doing, or what you can't do, or why you shouldn't do it. That is just putting other people's expectations on you, and could be that you are expressing a belief that you are not capable of doing it. Once you begin to hold your desire firmly in your mind, no matter what your negative thoughts or negative outside circumstances show, you will soon begin to see it all change.

How to Manifest through Emotions and Imagination

Remember I said that subconscious programming will emanate out to the universe and therefore, in reality, you will be fed back the same nonsense you have been telling yourself for years. This is only conditioning, and you can change it by understanding the Law of Attraction. If you follow my simple steps in the Workbook you will soon find that you begin your life today in a different frame of mind and will only attract good to you.

This is also important. When people feed this nonsense back to you, instead of arguing with them, don't react, as you will soon realise you are hearing this information because of the believable conditioning locked in your subconscious. Thus the universe is returning this message for you to see what your hidden messages to yourself are. If you cannot fully understand this, read it a few times until you hear the clear message.

> The less one reacts to a situation, over time the subconscious mind will pick up that you are in a serene vibration and this new vibration will most likely be detached from other people's emotions and opinions.
> Once this happens you will no longer find that their behaviour will cause a reaction inside of you, therefore you will not be affected by your outside circumstances. When you get to this point you will realise that you have mastered the gift of being in complete control of your destiny.

By this stage your ability to visualise your desires and bring about change in yourself is strong, therefore when you are in harmony with this knowing and new belief, you will tend to expect good and have faith that all wonderful opportunities in regards to your desire are becoming a reality. Faith is a state of mind which can be difficult to explain. FAITH is a result one attains by the persistence of repetition and action along with emotion and reprogramming the subconscious mind.

> *If you apply yourself on a daily basis to continually repeat affirmations with emotion,
> you will begin to believe your desire is becoming a reality; therefore when this chemical reaction occurs, what manifests on a higher consciousness is faith.*
>
> *You then have faith that your desire is manifesting so you stay in a constant state of detachment.
> You no longer express frustration,
> lack of anything and everything,
> or failure that you are losing in any way.
> Instead you have this knowing inside yourself
> that all is in divine order and you continue
> to move in the direction of your goals
> with absolute focus on where you are heading
> no matter what your outside
> circumstances appear to be.*

This is why desire, imagination and emotions play a vital role in living your purpose and fulfilling your desires. The way I look at it, is if you put everything you want into your subconscious mind and hold it firmly close to your heart and use all your emotions and imagination to create the image you desire, it is only a matter of time until the seed of your ideas manifest into reality. The faster you believe and hold your faith by focusing and taking action forward, the quicker the results will become reality.

> *Through your desire you will find you will never give up,
> and this is where persistence will take over.*

Anything new you desire, or anything you can imagine, is a new concept and that new concept only requires your desire to bring it into your reality.

> *New concepts are never proven
> until they are achieved;
> achievement is only our desire.*

With persistence you will always achieve your results and to keep being persistent is to continue to hold your desire close to your heart. When this desire becomes intense, you will only have one result to look forward to – and this is success in all you do.

Once you understand this power of your subconscious and experience the results from putting all this self-power into action, you know you have then mastered the Law of Attraction.

Now is the time to work with your extended Workbook, so make sure you have printed it out and continue this journey with me. If you have not got the file for the Workbook, please go back to my website **www.1-desire.com** to get your free copy.

Please follow instructions carefully as it is very important to do it in the right order. Before commencing with the workbook you must first read 'Prepare to Change Your Life' (Chapter Six) and then the Workbook introductions.

Chapter Six

Prepare to Change Your Life and Discover Your Hidden Self-sabotage/Paradigms

Firstly take a whole day to yourself, to be completely on your own. You will be asking yourself the first important question: "Why am I here?" This question is significant to all aspects of your life. Meaning: Why am I living here? Why am I in this relationship? Why am I in this job? Why am I having these health challenges? What is my ultimate passion in life? What do I want to achieve? What has been my experience? And so on. It is important to fill out all the answers in your exercise Workbook – it is keeping a diary of the steps you take in order for change.

Write each answer down with complete honesty. If you are not honest with yourself you will not gain the results you really desire in life. I say take a whole day because it will give you time to unlock the natural pattern you have had of doing and being with people to avoid being with yourself for too long. We always feel we need to fill an empty void so we latch on to others for comfort and find we can use them to push, prod and blame or even try to help and change their ways to suit ourselves. This is completely destructive and selfish to others and to ourselves. I am not saying we need to live a life of solitude; this is absolutely not what you are to do. You are to live a happy life, being close to others and having healthy relationships based on integrity, honesty and encompassing each individual to be the best they can be and to live the life each person deserves and was born to, without compromising who you are and what you were born to do. Before you can truly achieve this you must feel comfortable in your own skin and in your own space. Now, people who love their own space to the point where they don't want to be in a relationship also need to ask themselves a few questions. We are truly here to love and be loved.

Sometimes it is a matter of timing and growth from within as to when you are ready, and sometimes we make a conscious choice to stay single until we achieve something within ourselves before we can attract our lifelong partner. This is great to do, but at the same time we must bring attention to any issues about being in a relationship before we can grow. Some people have commitment issues because they don't want to get hurt, or they feel stifled, and some people just plainly believe they don't want to be tied down to one person all their life. All these reasons are clearly not coming from a pure heart space –fear stops our progress and we will never find true happiness this way.

One day you will wake up and realise you are alone and you have discovered the fact that you really wished you had shared your life with that someone special instead of having a partner out of mere loneliness and lack of independence. Let me assure you, you may have robbed yourself of this, but however long it has taken you to discover this, at least you have discovered it for your own growth to now move forward. Your life is still in perfection and all divine timing as it is meant to be. What is, is what is. You were responsible for making the choices to change or not to change.

Some of the questions you have to ask yourself can be unsettling as they really bring your truth to the surface. When you first take that step in taking a day for just yourself to find your true honesty, you may, surprisingly, have a lot of emotions arise and realisations which you may not have even consciously really known or confronted before. It is such a simple step to unlock your true destiny.

We only really choose change when we allow ourselves the opportunity to be completely honest with ourselves. We have to find who we are to be able to move forward. If we live our life in the dreams of others we will never be happy. If we live the life in the mindset of 'one day it will change', we will still find that day will never come. We have to want to change now. And to have reasons to want to change is your leverage. This is where undesired conditions have an important role in achieving results. When we associate a reason with our desired goal, this is what pushes us through to when we think we are at our limit of progress. All humans have that resistance point where they want to say 'okay, that's it, I have tried and failed'. Well be assured; you have failed only because you gave up.

> IT IS SIMPLE, JUST DON'T GIVE UP
> AND YOU WON'T EVER FAIL!

Learn From What is Going Wrong

If you are approaching a certain challenge in life the same way all the time and getting the same results, then bingo! There is your answer.

Everything that is going wrong in your life is because of the choices you have made. And if you find these choices were out of your control, maybe they *were* at that time. The only reason you did not have control then was because you were not aware you *could* take control of the situation. And you might now be saying to yourself: 'But I could not change the fact that so-and-so did this, or such-and-such happened here.' Well yes, not in that moment – you could have seen a different way to look at that situation, but what I am saying is that you had a choice about how to react to a bad situation. Now you must recognise that this instance may have occurred due to past choices, which is always what it comes down to. It is important to be aware of your destructive patterns that keep you experiencing the same situation, day in and day out. We choose certain things in our lives without knowing the outcome; however, why not just know the outcome? Of course, I don't mean go and find a fortune-teller.

After reading my book you should know exactly what I mean. Create your outcome. Use your imagination, thoughts and emotions. That way you will not always be struggling to make that one change.

As you find your way in learning to manifest your desires you will begin to set bigger and better goals, but this does not mean you will always have it go exactly how you want it. Life takes us on a journey about ourselves, and thus it is only to learn about our own growth. Our journey will always move in the direction of our desire if we keep that desire alive with focused, productive energy but it never appears to be in a straight line with the results. There are always twists and turns and people coming into our life for a reason to help with this flow. It may look positive and turn out negative, or vice versa. Anyway the situation that turns out is an opportunity for you to grow. Either way you end up winning, but only of course if you keep your eye on the prize and don't fall back into your old habits that keep you in the same place with the same reality.

Therefore it is of the utmost importance to know that you have the power to take control of your reality.

CHANGE YOUR APPROACH, WHICH WILL CHANGE YOUR RESULTS.

Life is to explore, and to explore we need to test all of the above which may work for us. Some people find it works certain ways for them, and some find what worked for others was not at all appropriate for them. You have to find what is right for you and what gives you motivation. When you have this motivation and enjoyment along the road of progress you will find you begin to achieve more and more on a continuous cycle. Just find your leverage and this is the key to achieving all you desire.

Sounds simple – maybe how simple depends on how much you choose to stay in victim consciousness and how much you desire something. I find desire is the key, it unlocks the strong emotion that impacts the subconscious mind, and in turn the subconscious mind creates your reality. The power of having a REASON changes everything. It gives you the drive to persist in achieving your desires.

Be Unrealistic and Realistic at the Same Time

Sounds confusing, yet this is a powerful key to moving forward with precise and clear focus.

What I mean by being unrealistic is using your imagination to dream up your ultimate desire.

This exercise is not unrealistic in relation to the Universal Laws; however, it may seem unrealistic to our practical mind and how we have been taught. It goes against everything we have learnt to believe in ourselves.

After following the Workbook exercises you will learn to allow yourself to imagine, and this is very important.

You must allow yourself every day to imagine your ultimate desire with emotion. This is the process of what people may call being in your unrealistic mind. But the key to it is to bring this image of desire into our reality. The way we do this is to move forward by taking action with realistic steps by being practical in our current reality. We must learn to expect our desire to manifest itself through our repetition of practical and realistic steps we take on a daily basis. We still need to stay grounded and take each step one at a time with precise focus. This is what I mean by being realistic to your current circumstances. For example it is not wise to go out and quit your job just because you are now meditating on your ultimate desire. The key is to make a gentle transition from your job into your desired reality. To do this you must continually move forward by taking progressive steps to get closer and closer to what you are imagining will become true for you. This imagination will turn into expectation, which is when you absolutely know it will happen, without a doubt.

When you believe in your desire and expect it, you are well on your way to success.

At this point we then begin to think ourselves worthy enough to desire to live how we were born to live.

I thank you for reading *Reclaim Your Subconscious Mind*, and I believe my Workbook can help you unlock your true potential by FINDING YOUR ULTIMATE DESIRE.

Don't forget to obtain a copy of your free Workbook at **www.1-desire.com**.

Each one of us is special and is born with a purpose to help others by shining our own light in whatever we desire to do. If you choose to fulfil your purpose, the impact you alone can have on the world is bigger than you realise. Energy shifts energy, and living your desire is very important, as when you live by example you can inspire others to change their lives, and the ripple effect continues to automatically help others do the same.

Abundance to you!

With gratitude
Marie Ireland

> I have given everything I have got,
> and now I will give it everything I forgot I had.

www.ingramcontent.com/pod-product-compliance
Lightning Source LLC
Chambersburg PA
CBHW071307040426
42444CB00009B/1913